IT'S TIME TO EAT PRICKLY PEARS

It's Time to Eat
PRICKLY PEARS

Walter the Educator

Silent King Books
A WhichHead Entertainment Imprint

Copyright © 2025 by Walter the Educator

All rights reserved. No part of this book may be reproduced in any manner whatsoever without written per- mission except in the case of brief quotations embodied in critical articles and reviews.

First Printing, 2024

Disclaimer

This book is a literary work; the story is not about specific persons, locations, situations, and/or circumstances unless mentioned in a historical context. Any resemblance to real persons, locations, situations, and/or circumstances is coincidental. This book is for entertainment and informational purposes only. The author and publisher offer this information without warranties expressed or implied. No matter the grounds, neither the author nor the publisher will be accountable for any losses, injuries, or other damages caused by the reader's use of this book. The use of this book acknowledges an understanding and acceptance of this disclaimer.

It's Time to Eat PRICKLY PEARS is a collectible early learning book by Walter the Educator suitable for all ages belonging to Walter the Educator's Time to Eat Book Series. Collect more books at WaltertheEducator.com

USE THE EXTRA SPACE TO TAKE NOTES AND DOCUMENT YOUR MEMORIES

PRICKLY PEARS

It's time to eat, the treat is here,

It's Time to Eat Prickly Pears

A fruit so bright, the prickly pear!

It's juicy, sweet, and such a sight,

With colors bold, red, green, and bright.

On cactus tall, it loves to grow,

With tiny spines, so watch them, though!

We wear our gloves and take great care,

To safely pick the prickly pear.

The spines come off, and then we peel,

To see the fruit, it's quite the deal!

Inside, it's soft and pink or red,

A yummy treat to keep us fed.

We slice it up or make a juice,

Or mix it up in tasty mousse.

It's good in jams or sweet desserts,

With every bite, our hunger hurts.

It's Time to Eat
Prickly Pears

The seeds inside are small and round,

You crunch them up, they make a sound!

Or spit them out into the breeze,

It's fun to eat it as you please.

The taste is sweet, a little tart,

It's healthy too, so good for heart.

With every bite, the day feels bright,

A prickly pear is pure delight!

We share it round, with family near,

A special snack to bring us cheer.

The cactus fruit, a treasure rare,

We all enjoy this prickly pear!

Let's thank the sun, the rain, the earth,

For helping grow this fruity worth.

Nature's gift, both wild and free,

It's Time to Eat
Prickly Pears

The prickly pear's a joy for me!

Now let's all smile and munch away,

This treat has made a perfect day.

With sticky hands and happy cheer,

We'll eat them all, then wait next year.

So when you see a cactus bloom,

And fruits that grow in bright costume,

Remember then this joyful care

It's Time to Eat
Prickly Pears

It's time to eat a prickly pear!

ABOUT THE CREATOR

Walter the Educator is one of the pseudonyms for Walter Anderson. Formally educated in Chemistry, Business, and Education, he is an educator, an author, a diverse entrepreneur, and he is the son of a disabled war veteran. "Walter the Educator" shares his time between educating and creating. He holds interests and owns several creative projects that entertain, enlighten, enhance, and educate, hoping to inspire and motivate you. Follow, find new works, and stay up to date with Walter the Educator™

at WaltertheEducator.com

www.ingramcontent.com/pod-product-compliance
Lightning Source LLC
LaVergne TN
LVHW052014060526
838201LV00059B/4027